THE ETHICAL TRAVELLER

IMOGEN LEPERE

THE ETHICAL TRAVELLER

100 ways to roam the world
(WITHOUT RUINING IT!)

Smith
Street
Books

INTRODUCTION

When I told a friend in Melbourne that I was writing a book about ethical travel, he said the two things I suspect many of you are thinking: 'Whenever I think about social inequality and the climate crisis, I feel completely overwhelmed,' and 'Isn't the idea of ethical travel kinda hypocritical bullsh*t?' We were on the phone and he was walking along the creek from Coburg to Northcote in Melbourne, so we had a few minutes. Here's what I told him.

In 2015, leaders from the 193 countries that make up the United Nations came together to create an ambitious plan that became known as the Sustainable Development Goals. This set of seventeen aims provided a vision of the future where extreme poverty and hunger don't exist, where we're safe from the worst effects of climate change and the gap between rich and poor is shrinking. The deadline? 2030. It's ambitious, yes, but not impossible. Between 2000 and 2015, the global community cut extreme poverty in half. Who says we can't try to finish the job?

American women's rights activist Lotte E. Scharfman once said, 'Democracy is not a spectator sport.' Well, making the Sustainable Development Goals happen isn't either. Travel provides countless opportunities to play your part – both big and small.

Yes, travel and flying in particular does cause carbon emissions (although there are tips to mitigate this in this very book). However, tourism also creates one out of every ten jobs globally. Many of these are in remote corners where communities play a crucial role in protecting delicate ecosystems and ways of life. Others allow those on the margins to gain independence in societies where that is far from a given.

Travel can be one of many pathways to making our planet a safer, fairer and kinder place – somewhere people and nature thrive in harmony. Here's how to see the world while helping to save it, one trip at a time.

Imogen Lepere
LONDON, UK

HOW TO USE
THIS BOOK

Make this book work for you.

Think of this book as a pocket-sized wheelie suitcase – granted it's far, far cuter thanks to Julia Murray's illustrations. Whether you have a strict packing system or prefer to pull clothes out of your closet at random, it does the heavy lifting for you.

Now that I've pushed that metaphor as far (maybe further?) than it needs to go, we can get down to business. Tips are organised in an order that loosely represents the stages of travel – planning, packing, getting there, being away and leaving a positive legacy – but diving in at random works just as well.

The icons on each page signify which Sustainable Development Goal (SDG) the tip aligns with – you can find a complete list opposite. If there's a particular goal you feel passionate about, focus on tips that help make it a reality. Simple.

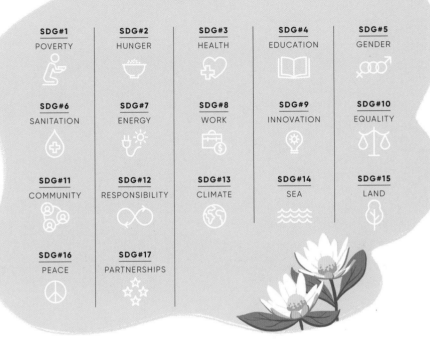

SDG#1 POVERTY	SDG#2 HUNGER	SDG#3 HEALTH	SDG#4 EDUCATION	SDG#5 GENDER
SDG#6 SANITATION	SDG#7 ENERGY	SDG#8 WORK	SDG#9 INNOVATION	SDG#10 EQUALITY
SDG#11 COMMUNITY	SDG#12 RESPONSIBILITY	SDG#13 CLIMATE	SDG#14 SEA	SDG#15 LAND
SDG#16 PEACE	SDG#17 PARTNERSHIPS			

SUSTAINABLE DEVELOPMENT GOAL BY TIPS

SDG#1 Poverty (tips 06, 37, 70, 75)

SDG#2 Hunger (tips 27, 68, 69, 71, 72)

SDG#3 Health (tips 09, 28, 40, 76, 81, 82, 92)

SDG#4 Education (tips 11, 41, 45)

SDG#5 Gender (tips 05, 46, 83, 84, 98)

SDG#6 Sanitation (tips 15, 32, 33, 44)

SDG#7 Energy (tips 10, 16, 17, 19, 20, 21, 22, 26, 39, 85)

SDG#8 Work (tips 01, 02, 07, 08, 47, 77, 97)

SDG#9 Innovation (tips 04, 23, 48, 54, 64, 86)

SDG#10 Equality (tips 49, 73, 94, 95)

SDG#11 Community (tips 24, 29, 30, 35, 42, 43, 52, 53, 87)

SDG#12 Responsibility (tips 12, 13, 14, 18, 34, 36, 74, 78, 79, 80)

SDG#13 Climate (tips 03, 31, 67, 93)

SDG#14 Sea (tips 56, 57, 58, 59, 60, 88)

SDG#15 Land (tips 50, 51, 55, 61, 62, 89, 96)

SDG#16 Peace (tips 25, 63, 65, 66, 90, 91)

SDG#17 Partnerships (tips 38, 99)

01

TAKE THE ROAD
LESS TRAVELLED

LIKE THE FAMOUS ACTOR WHO ENDS UP BEING TYPECAST, OVERTOURISM
turns certain destinations into parodies of themselves. Just look at central
Venice pre-Covid, where bumper-to-bumper gondolas and restaurants
serving frozen bolognaise for €30 a pop came as standard. As well as
leading to inauthentic experiences for travellers, too much tourism decimates
local ecosystems and makes daily life nigh on impossible for locals. It's far
better to pick a region's second, third or even fourth city instead. Think skiing
in Bulgaria's Rila Mountains instead of the Swiss Alps, browsing Rotterdam's
galleries instead of joining the crush in Amsterdam, or strolling along Treviso's
canals instead of Venice's.

CONSIDER WHERE YOU ARE MOST NEEDED

APPROACH YOUR HOLIDAY PLANNING STRATEGICALLY SO YOU CAN PICK somewhere that really needs your support. Disaster Tourism may sound gross but the aftermath of a natural disaster or terrorist attack is when your dollars are needed the most. It's also important to engage with destinations that are dealing with negative publicity and tell your friends the real story — if it is safe to do so, of course. Other destinations where your money means more are those that are highly dependent on tourism. Take the tiny Caribbean Islands of Antigua and Barbuda, where visiting beach-lovers bolster 90% of the local economy.

03

PICK AN ECO-FRIENDLY DESTINATION

SOME DESTINATIONS SHOW A LOT MORE LOVE FOR THE PLANET THAN others. Here are three shining examples:

* **Costa Rica** – Costa Rica disbanded its army in 1948 and redirected the money into conservation, health and education. Today more than 99% of its energy comes from renewable resources and its emerald jungles are home to almost 6% of the world's animal and plant species.

* **Slovenia** – With more than half its surface covered in forest and 13% of its landscape protected, this almost landlocked country is like Europe's green heart. Cycle between red-roofed villages exploring castles, spot bears in the Alps, and bathe in mineral-rich mountain streams.

* **Sweden** – A long-time leader in the sustainable travel game, Stockholm's public transport system is mostly electric and its residents are passionate about urban farming. Away from the city, glorious forests and fjords offer hiking and foraging opportunities aplenty.

GIVE HIGH SEASON
THE COLD SHOULDER

LOWER PRICES, FEWER CROWDS AND A WARMER WELCOME ARE JUST A few reasons to travel during the off-season. In spots that struggle with overtourism – the point at which the needs of the tourism industry become unsustainable for a destination – resources such as water and transport may become harder for locals to access. Low season can be wonderfully atmospheric (picture Venice's deserted backstreets in January mist), while 'shoulder season' – those months between high and low – may actually provide preferable weather. Hiking Crete's Kydoni Gorge, for example, is far more enjoyable in May, when the floor is carpeted with wild herbs and temperatures are a comfortable 21 degrees Celsius (70 degrees Fahrenheit).

05

FREE YOUR INNER EXPLORER ON A SOLO TRIP

ALTHOUGH FEMALE ADVENTURERS HAVE BEEN TRAVELLING FOR centuries, most of the names we know belong to men (hello again, Captain Cook). Google has reported that searches for the term 'solo travel' almost tripled between 2015 and 2020 and, according to industry reports, 85% of those travellers are women. Cosmopolitan cities like Bangkok and London seem to be favourite destinations, but if you're interested in visiting somewhere more remote, small group tours can be a great way of meeting new friends and sidestepping all the research. Intrepid (*intrepidtravel.com*) is the world's largest carbon-neutral travel company and group sizes are never more than 10. They also offer a range of women-only tours.

06

MAKE YOURSELF AT HOME

WITH ON-SITE RESTAURANTS AND 24/7 SERVICE, A HOTEL BELONGING TO an international group can feel like the safe option. But isn't breaking free of your comfort zone part of travel? Opt for a homestay and you'll have a far more memorable experience – as well as making sure 100% of your money benefits your hosts, rather than being syphoned out of the local economy by an international company. Browse global sites like Homestay (*homestay.com*) or see if the specific region you're visiting has its own version. For example, Your Home In Japan (*yourhomeinjapan.com*) covers Tokyo, Look After Me (*lookafterme.co.nz*) is the equivalent in New Zealand, and Homestay Ireland (*homestayireland.ie*) has rural options in Ireland.

07

BE AWARE OF GREENWASHING

MANY MORE PEOPLE CARE ABOUT CREATING A SUSTAINABLE FUTURE AND understand that every dollar or Euro they spend could be seen as a vote for the kind of world they want to live in. Unfortunately, those canny folks in the marketing department have also spotted this, which is why communications in the tourism industry are filled with 'greenwashing'. Look out for vague claims without stats to back them up, no sign of locals on an operators' social media channels, no mention of independent businesses, and claims that they align with specific Sustainable Development Goals (SDGs) just by the nature of what they do. If you suspect, snitch! Press the company for more details and if none are provided, report them to that country's tourism board.

CHECK THE HR POLICY TOO

A HOTEL OR TRAVEL COMPANY SHOULD BE ONLY TOO HAPPY TO TOOT their own horn about their recruitment policy if it's ethical, so double check the sustainability page on their website before booking. If unclear, ask. Hotels with fair recruitment policies can do a huge amount of good, particularly if they're in a country where it has traditionally been tricky for women or people of minority ethnicities to find work. If booking through an operator, be sure to check that guides are offered training and insurance – they deserve it.

09

OPT FOR ETHICAL TRAVEL INSURANCE

ALONG WITH VISA FORMS AND AIRPORT FOOD, FINDING THE RIGHT insurance is one of the less exciting parts of going abroad. Yet, it is a must on every ethical traveller's to-do list. Get a policy that includes premium healthcare so you won't burden underfunded local facilities, and look for a provider that shouts about the fact it doesn't invest in fossil fuels.

THE GOOD, BAD AND UGLY OF CARBON OFFSETTING

IN THEORY, CARBON OFFSETS HELP BALANCE YOUR CARBON FOOTPRINT by funding environmental projects that reduce greenhouse gases in the atmosphere. One carbon offset credit equals one metric tonne of carbon dioxide removed from the air. Sounds pretty good, huh? The trouble is that nature-based offsetting (i.e. planting trees) relies heavily on land in the global south where people are already struggling with the impacts of the climate crisis and do not produce nearly as much carbon as the wealthy West. This land is often seized from Indigenous groups or planted with uniform trees that can't support biodiversity in the way a natural forest can. Look out for carbon offset schemes with a Gold Standard (*goldstandard.org*) certification to be sure your money is helping rather than hindering but remember, it's always better to reduce carbon emissions than offset them.

PACK WITH PURPOSE

IT'S TEMPTING TO FILL EVERY CRANNY OF YOUR BAG WITH THOSE
holiday clothes you never actually wear but leaving a little room for school
supplies will ultimately make you feel even more fabulous. Pack for a Purpose
(*packforapurpose.org*) is a not-for-profit that connects travellers with schools
and community projects in their travel destination so they can bring the
supplies that are actually needed. Worried about squishing it all in? Start
by removing packaging and use the KonMari (*konmari.com*) method to fold
your clothes.

... AND KEEP IT LIGHT

DID YOU KNOW THAT THE LIGHTER YOUR BAG, THE FEWER CO$_2$ EMISSIONS produced by your flight? According to the UN's Environment Programme, reducing the weight of your luggage by 15 kg (33 lbs) decreases your emissions by around 50–100 kg (110–220 lbs) on a four-and-a-half-hour flight.

13

LEAVE PACKAGING AT HOME

YOU'RE IN A TENT IN TANZANIA WITH THE SOUNDS OF THE SERENGETI seeping through the canvas. Time for some mosquito repellent... but what to do with the plastic seal? Recycling facilities in remote destinations are usually far harder to access than at home, so be sure to cut off all tags and ditch boxes before you go.

RENTING IS THE NEW NEW

FROM DESIGNER SUNHATS TO CAMPING EQUIPMENT, CHANCES ARE YOU can rent everything you need for your holiday. Not only is it cheaper and smarter when it comes to saving precious cupboard space, it also means you can enjoy the novelty of 'new to you' goods every time you go away without creating waste. It's the perfect chance to see if paisley really is your print after all.

15

ECO-PROOF YOUR HOME

CONSOLIDATE ALL THE EFFORT YOU'VE PUT INTO PLANNING AN ETHICAL holiday by giving your home a once over before you go. As a start:

- find the stop tap and turn it off to prevent leaks (as well as defend against floods if there were some sort of plumbing failure);
- unplug electronic devices, especially those with a standby mode as these guzzle energy; and
- put the thermostat on eco mode or turn it off if it isn't winter.

BECOME AN AIRLINE ACTIVIST

WE DO GET IT: BECAUSE YOU'RE PRESSED FOR TIME OR TRAVELLING long-haul, flying is sometimes the only viable option. Don't beat yourself up about it. Instead, use Skyscanner's (*skyscanner.net*) 'greener choice' filter when you search and once you've chosen a flight, head over to Atmosfair (*fairfuel.atmosfair.de*) to work out the carbon cost of your trip and offset it. Sustainable aviation fuel is being researched all over the world and Air Transport Action Group (*atag.org*) is your one-stop-shop to learn all about the latest news and find out which destinations are leading the charge. Oslo Airport was the first international hub to offer biofuel to all departing airlines, while Israeli company, Eviation, is hoping to bring electric passenger planes to the market in 2024. Watch this space...

TIP#

17

SDG#7

ENERGY

BE A PEOPLE PERSON

SORRY PERSONAL-SPACE FANS, BUT IF YOU MUST FLY, PLEASE MAKE SURE it's in economy. Studies show emissions per passenger in first class can be nine times as much as the good people at the back, with business passengers coming in at three times the emissions of those in economy. This is simply because more people + a smaller space = greater fuel efficiency.

JOIN THE RESPONSIBLE MILE HIGH CLUB

THE AIR TRANSPORT ASSOCIATION SAYS THAT PASSENGERS ON FLIGHTS collectively generate 5.7 million tonnes of cabin waste every year. That's more weight than 150,000 humpback whales! Bringing your own blanket, food, water bottle, socks, toothbrush and pyjamas will ensure a more comfortable journey as well as making a significant dent in the single-use plastics generated by your trip. Oh, and remember to charge your phone so you don't end up having to print paperwork at the airport. This ain't 2002.

19

STAY ON THE RAILS

THERE'S NO DOUBT A TRAIN IS ALWAYS MORE CARBON-EFFICIENT THAN A flight but not all trains are created equal. Electric trains, like those that whisk people around Sydney and Moscow, typically generate up to 35% less carbon per kilometre than their diesel equivalents. In the Netherlands, passenger trains run on wind power and Chile's Santiago Metro relies mostly on its own solar plant. In Europe, Germany is leading the way when it comes to renewable rail travel. The world's first hydrogen-powered passenger trains are currently speeding silently between Buxtehude and the beach town of Cuxhaven several times a day.

20

SHARING IS CARING

SOME OF THE WORLD'S GREATEST LITERATURE HAS BEEN WRITTEN ABOUT road trips — think authors such as F. Scott Fitzgerald, Jack Kerouac, Marcel Proust — but the reality can often be more gridlock-and-bad-snack-stop than soul-stirring vistas and wind in your hair. Using a ride-sharing app, such as PopaRide (*poparide.com*) in Canada and BlaBlaCar (*blablacar.co.uk*), available in 22 European countries, not only cuts carbon emissions, it also offers you the chance to chat with locals in a low-pressure, egalitarian environment. In a recent poll, 87% of BlaBlaCar users said that they'd had an enriching exchange with their peers, with 84% saying they'd learned something new during the ride.

TAKE FAIRER FERRIES

TYPICALLY, PASSENGER FERRIES HAVE RUN ON 'BUNKER FUEL' WHICH IS about as good for the environment as it sounds. However, a new fleet of sustainably minded boats are leaving the harbour and steering us towards calmer seas. Say, 'Ahoy' to:

- Wasaline's (*wasaline.com*) hybrid *Aurora Botnia* ship between Vaasa in Finland and Umeå in Sweden, which runs on liquefied natural gas and battery power;
- Pentland Ferries' (*pentlandferries.co.uk*) MV *Alfred*, which glides from Scotland's Caithness to Orkney Island using 60% less fuel than standard ferries thanks to its twin hull.

WHAT ABOUT ELECTRIC CARS?

ALL THE BIG CAR RENTAL COMPANIES OFFER ELECTRIC, INCLUDING Europcar, SIXT and Hertz, and many cities are also buzzing with fleets of electric taxis ready to whizz you from A to B. Uber Green can be found in major cities across Canada and North America as well as London, while Mexico City's Beat uses electric Tesla cars. Buckle up and enjoy the ride.

23

LET'S GO PUBLIC

AN ELECTRIC CAR MAY HAVE LOWER EMISSIONS THAN MANY FORMS OF public transport but going public is often more ethical due to the huge pressure tourism can put on roads. Take the Hawaiian island of Maui. Its famous Hana Highway is an important route for local people to travel between Hana and Kaupo, but as it winds between waterfalls and lush green cliffs, it also attracts 2,000 rental cars and 100 tour buses per day in high season. Traffic and inconsiderate parking means locals have to drive a back route to get essentials from shops or travel to work, adding up to two hours to their journey. Opting for public transport rather than hiring your own vehicle will save you money, too.

ACCESS ACCESSIBLE TRAVEL

THE WORLD HEALTH ORGANIZATION ESTIMATES THAT AT LEAST 15% OF THE world's population has some form of disability – that equates to around 1 billion people, many of whom are hungry to experience the life-enhancing benefits of travel. The industry has been slow to recognise this and has typically been inflexible on things like excessive fees when debilitating symptoms force postponement or failing to offer exciting alternatives if certain activities are out of reach. So, let's give a resounding huzzah to the operators dedicated to getting travellers with disabilities on the road. Here are two examples:

- **Wheel the World** (*gowheeltheworld.com*) organises multi-day trips in partnership with local tour operators with a focus on accessible travel and they also have a large directory of accessible hotels including details like bed heights. Prices are the same whether the traveller has a disability or not.
- **Planet Abled** (*planetabled.com*) arranges customised tours for people with differing abilities throughout India and Southeast Asia. Some of their extra touches include assigning a travel buddy for the vision impaired and arranging sign language interpreters for the hearing impaired.

25

SUPPORT THE TOURIST TAX

MORE THAN 50 COUNTRIES HAVE A TOURIST TAX, OFTEN PAYABLE alongside your visa or as part of a plane ticket. It can feel irksome to have to shell out on top of your holiday spend but it's a great way to contribute to the infrastructure your visit may put extra pressure on, like roads and healthcare. Some destinations, such as Palau, Bhutan and Galapagos, have 'green fees' – tourist taxes that go towards conservation – and these destinations are often leading the way in conservation.

SUPPORT HOTELS THAT HAVE GONE GREEN

IF A HOTEL IS TALKING THE GREEN TALK, IT SHOULD BE WALKING THE renewable energy walk – that means a large proportion of its energy being generated by renewable sources such as solar, wind or hydropower. Many hotels are climate positive these days, meaning they create more energy than they use. Coco Hotel, a boutique bolthole in Copenhagen, has its own solar farm, while in French Polynesia, The Brando has a pioneering air-conditioning system that harnesses the coolness of sea water to reduce energy demands by more than 40%. Now that is truly cool.

INDULGE YOUR FARM FANTASY

WANT TO IMMERSE YOURSELF IN NATURE WHILE HELPING RURAL communities thrive? Hitting the hay on a farm gives small-scale farmers some extra cash — and you the chance to try your hand (or foot) at things like grape stomping and bottle-feeding lambs. If you have more time, consider volunteering as a WWOOFer (*wwoof.com*); you'll get free accommodation and board in exchange for working on an organic farm. A checked shirt and overalls are optional but highly recommended.

CHECK IN TO HEALTHY HOTELS

DAZZLING SUNSETS AND CLEAN, CRISP AIR MAKES STAYING IN REMOTE hotels feel like a boon for our health so make sure you're prioritising those that care about the health of their community too. Take Shakti, which operates walking tours in the Kumaon region of the Indian Himalayas and introduced modern plumbing to the area. They also run regular medical camps where villagers can get treatments and learn more about sanitation.

(UNF)AIRBNB

WHEN FOUNDERS JOE GEBBIA AND BRIAN CHESKY RENTED OUT THREE AIR mattresses in their living room during a San Francisco design conference in 2007, no one could have predicted what would follow. This is the origin story of Airbnb, the peer-to-peer accommodation platform that has since changed the face of travel. By 2021, more than 7 million listings in 220 countries were making travel more affordable and accessible – for travellers that is. In cities that suffer from overtourism, such as Paris, Amsterdam and Barcelona, short-term lets have caused skyrocketing rents that displace locals. What few people realise is that many of these are, in fact, breaking the law: in New York, it's illegal to rent entire apartments to tourists for less than 30 days without a licence yet NYC is one of the most popular cities on the platform. Do your research and, if necessary, opt for a locally owned guesthouse, hostel or serviced apartment instead.

30

ETHICAL AIRBNB ALTERNATIVES

'SURE, HOTELS AND GUESTHOUSES ARE GREAT, BUT I WANT TO EXPERIENCE a destination like a local,' we hear you cry. Fear not. In places that don't struggle with too much tourism, or if you're renting a spare room rather than a whole apartment, Airbnb isn't a problem. However, there are plenty of other peer-to-peer platforms to consider. Here are a couple of our favourites:

* **Fairbnb** (*fairbnb.coop*) was partly developed by a panel of European citizens concerned about the negative impacts of Airbnb. Hosts must be local and can only list one property each, while 50% of the platform's fees go towards community projects.

* **Ecobnb** (*ecobnb.com*) offers accommodation that fulfils 10 criteria including car-free access, 100% renewable energy, organic food, and recycling more than 80% of their waste. Current listings include a farmhouse overlooking a deserted beach in Corinthia, Greece and a Tuscan villa nestled among organic vines.

31

GET ON BOARD WITH OVERLANDING

THE IDEA THAT TRAVELLING IS MORE ABOUT THE JOURNEY THAN THE destination might be a cliché, but there is good reason for that. Often the most memorable interactions from a trip will be the times you rubbed shoulders with locals, and public transport is one of the most accessible – and cost-effective – ways to do just that. Eschew internal flights in favour of buses, boats and trains and you'll truly see the country you're visiting, rather than just its highlights reel. Piecing together a public transport route can take longer; if you're short on time, try to find a way of working from the road. Think of travel as a form of meditation: watch the sun rise over mountains, chat to the school children on the bus and share your snacks with the person on the next seat. You're guaranteed to have some stories to tell if you do.

KEEP SHOWERS SHORT

YOU HEARD IT HERE FIRST PEOPLE: BATHS ARE OVER, PARTICULARLY IN countries with water scarcity, which affects more than 40% of the world's population. Opt for shorter showers and bathing in good karma instead. Another easy win is enquiring whether a hotel has low-flow showerheads and re-uses wastewater in its gardens. Many do but if the answer's no, at least you've started a conversation.

DO NOT FORGET YOUR
DO NOT DISTURB SIGN

THE AVERAGE HOTEL GUEST USES AN ESTIMATED 100–200 GALLONS
of water daily, mostly caused by having their linens and towels washed every
day. Aside from being your best pal when it comes to lie-ins, the Do Not
Disturb sign is your secret weapon. Hang it on the door on the days you don't
really need housekeeping and you're a greener guest already.

RETHINK TOILETRIES

IN THE PAST, THOSE CUTE BOTTLES OF TOILETRIES WERE ONE OF THE
most novel things about staying at a fancy hotel. Doing 'the sweep' – that
last-minute swipe of surfaces to bundle every freebie into your suitcase – felt
like a rite of passage, never mind the fact they eventually ended up in the
bin after years of crowding your bathroom shelves. They also account for
a significant percentage of the hotel industry's single-use plastics. Instead,
invest in a few refillable bottles that come in below 100 ml (3½ fl oz) so you
can top up with what you have at home and take them in hand luggage. Even
better, opt for solid shampoo and soap bars that come in biodegradable
packaging.

35

KEEP IT COMMUNITY-LED

WHO BETTER TO WELCOME YOU INTO AN INDIGENOUS COMMUNITY THAN the people who live there? When communities run their own lodges or tour companies you can be sure that every penny is helping them thrive, and that your peek into their culture is the real deal rather one staged for tourists. Try:

- **Wiwa Tours** (*wiwatour.com*), offering treks through Colombia's isolated Sierra Nevada de Santa Marta mountains, staying at Indigenous-owned camps along the way.
- **Caiman House** (*caimanhouse.com*) in Guyana, which is owned and run by Yupukari Village. You can help local Amerindian people collect data and tag caimans along the Rupununi River.
- **Ngaran Ngaran Cultural Awareness** (*ngaranaboriginalculture.com*), run two-day retreats in NSW, Australia where travellers explore Djirringanj country, heartland of the Yuin people, as well as listening to their sacred Dreaming stories. Accommodation is in simple glamping tents while menus celebrate native produce and Indigenous cooking techniques.

SLEEP WITH AS MANY PEOPLE AS POSSIBLE

WE'RE TALKING DORM ROOMS HERE – WHY, WHAT DID YOU THINK WE meant? Hostel dorms are way better for the environment than standard doubles or self-catered apartments because utilities are shared. They're also easier on the wallet and a great chance to meet cool people, particularly if you're a solo traveller.

37

ASK A LOCAL TO SHOW YOU ROUND

THE STATUE WHERE VILLAGE CHILDREN GO TO MAKE WISHES; THE HOLE-
in-the-wall bakery that sells the wobbliest pastéis de nata (Portuguese
custard tarts); the valley that floods in certain weather conditions – aside
from being able to go below the surface of a destination, local guides are
normally better equipped to handle unexpected bumps in the road. Support
them wherever possible and if booking through an international operator,
always ask about their recruitment policies. Shiroube (*shiroube.com*) covers
more than 3,000 cities and has functions allowing you to search by language
as well as interest, while I Like Local (*i-likelocal.com*) is a sustainable travel
marketplace that lets you book positive experiences in Africa and Asia.

TALK THE TALK

OF THE APPROXIMATELY 1.5 BILLION PEOPLE WHO SPEAK ENGLISH IN THE world, less than 400 million use it as a first language. If one billion four hundred and ninety-six million people can learn a second language, surely we can have a crack too, even if it's just a few key words or phrases while travelling. Apps like Duolingo, Babbel and Memrise can provide the basics and are a constructive way to fill time at the airport or if you find yourself held up.

39

TAP INTO YOUR OWN GREEN ENERGY

WHAT'S THE CLEANEST ENERGY YOU CAN USE TO EXPLORE A NEW PLACE?
Your own of course! Whether 'bikepacking' Tasmania's Arthur Range, cycling around Taipei, or spending a long weekend in one of Portugal's many strollable cities, the fact is that getting around under your own steam is always preferable from an environmental point of view. It is also an excellent way to immerse yourself in a new place. Many cities offer guided walking tours or self-guided routes for free. Check out Melbourne's self-guided street art route from Melbourne City Council (*whatson.melbourne.vic.gov.au*).

SDG#3
HEALTH

TIP#

40

REDIRECT YOUR INNER MARY POPPINS

ALTHOUGH SPENDING A DAY VOLUNTEERING WITH ORPHANS SOUNDS great, the reality is that it's disruptive at best and at worst, encourages exploitation. All too often orphanage owners have convinced vulnerable parents to send their children away in exchange for money. If we aren't qualified to work with children in our own country, we aren't overseas either. For more tips on keeping kids safe while travelling, consult Child Safe Movement (*thinkchildsafe.org*).

BE OPEN TO LIFE LESSONS

IT'S SO EASY TO GET SUCKED INTO CHASING THE NEXT PAY RISE OR scrambling up the property ladder but listening to people who have different values reminds us to constantly reassess our own. Here are two poignant life lessons from around the world:

- **Wabi sabi, Japan** – Wabi translates as 'simplicity' and sabi, 'the beauty of age and wear', something that can be hard to wrap our heads around in our ageist culture. Wabi sabi captures the idea that accepting – and celebrating – imperfection and transience is a key step towards finding happiness.
- **Dolce far niente, Italy** – Meaning 'the sweetness of doing nothing', this attitude is what sees Romans clocking off work at 5pm to sip spritz in the piazzas, or letting lunch roll on for hours. It's about accepting that life is mostly out of our control and therefore we might as well kick back and enjoy the ride.

FANCY A DATE?

DATING APPS – TINDER IN PARTICULAR – CAN BE AN AMAZING WAY TO make connections on the road. There are few more effective ways to meet people quickly, especially if you aren't staying in a hostel. The important thing is being transparent about what you're looking for and how long you'll be sticking around in your bio, so other users only match with you if they're on the same page. Whether you're after the one, travel buddies, tour guides, or to do a language swap, you may be surprised by how many people are searching for the same thing.

43

HELLO STRANGER

CONNECTING WITH OTHERS IS A POWERFUL TOOL TO FOSTER A SHARED sense of responsibility. How could someone not want to act on the rising temperatures that recently caused famine in Madagascar when they've just spent an afternoon playing *fanorona* (a board game) with an old man in the shade of a baobab tree? Always have a smile to offer and a hand ready for a fist pump or shake. If you have food on a journey, ask the person next to you if they're hungry. Try couch surfing (*couchsurfing.com*) and Meetup (*meetup. com*) to connect with like-minded locals. Strangers really can be just friends you haven't met yet.

44

ANSWER THE CALL OF NATURE ... YES, *THAT* CALL

WE'VE ALL BEEN THERE: OUT HIKING, JUST GETTING A SECOND WIND AND suddenly... desperate to pee. According to the Leave No Trace Center for Outdoor Ethics (*lnt.org*) there's nothing wrong with 'copping a squat' as long as that squat is 200 metres – or 70 big steps – away from the nearest water source to avoid contamination. If we're dealing with number twos, our best bet is to dig a hole the depth of a hand and a half and use biodegradable toilet paper (which breaks down five times quicker than standard). Sorry wilderness lovers, that does mean carrying a trowel if you think you might get caught short.

GET AN A+ FOR VOLUNTEERING

WHILE WE ALL KNOW EDUCATION IS ONE OF THE MOST SURE-FIRE WAYS to change the world, kids aren't tourist attractions and good intentions alone do not a teacher make. So, how to engage with schools in an ethical way? If you have skills to share but are short on time, offer to run a workshop for staff instead. If you can commit to several months, choose your volunteering program carefully. A good one should offer pre-departure child protection training and be transparent about what percentage of your fee goes to the school or project.

SPOT THE INVISIBLE WOMEN

LOOK OUT FOR OPPORTUNITIES TO SUPPORT WOMEN EMPLOYED IN travel jobs that have stereotypically been seen as 'belonging' to men, such as porters, guides and drivers. It might take a little extra digging but seek and ye shall find. Non-profit Planeterra (*planeterra.org*) champions community tourism enterprises led by women, including Wheels for Women, which has so far trained 1,000 female cab drivers across India, and the Pink City Rickshaw Company, your go-to for rickshaw tours of Jaipur. Where do we sign up?

47

EMBRACE THE UNDERDOG

OPT FOR EXPERIENCES THAT DIRECTLY SUPPORT SOMEONE WHO HAS faced challenges, gives them an economic boost, and helps to debunk stigmas and overcome social divisions. Look out for initiatives like Refugee Voices' (*refugeevoicestours.org*) walking tours of Berlin, Interno (*restauranteinterno.com*), a fine dining restaurant in Cartagena's San Diego women's prison, and Shades Tours (*shades-tours.com*), where a homeless person will educate you about how the social system works as they show you around Vienna's soup kitchens and shelters.

CHAT TO LOCALS

ISAAC NEWTON MAY CREDIT AN APPLE FOR HELPING HIM DEVELOP THE theory of gravity, but we'll wager that most innovations come from conversation. This is why it's so important to chat to locals rather than exclusively to other travellers. Next time you're in a bar or café, look for opportunities to spark up conversation. You may find you're helping to spark new ideas too.

GIVE THE RIGHT GIFTS

BRINGING GIFTS TO REMOTE COMMUNITIES PROVIDES LOCALS WITH A glimpse into a culture they may never visit and can make the whole experience feel like a meaningful exchange rather than a photo opportunity. Although many travellers want to bring sweets for children, remember that they won't necessarily have access to dental care and are often short of the bare necessities. Speak to your guide or tour operator about what might be needed before you leave home, and when you arrive hand everything over to the village elder rather than distributing things willy-nilly. They'll be in a far better position to make sure your gifts go to those who'll benefit most.

RESPECT WILDLIFE

YES, SOME ZOOS AND AQUARIUMS ARE DOING IMPORTANT RESEARCH, BUT animals were born to be wild (so the song goes). You should be highly suspicious of any operators offering the chance to get too close to wildlife, let alone touch it. We've all seen photos of folks in Thailand posing beside tigers who've consumed more drugs than the crowd at Glastonbury. Or riding elephants in India. We get it, a social media–worthy shot has a strong pull, but elephants' spines can't support humans and riding them results in serious injuries. Don't contribute to the suffering of the very creatures you've come to see. Instead, seek out non-profits that promote conservation and education.

WALK ON THE (RE)WILD SIDE

REWILDING – THE RESTORATION OF ECOSYSTEMS TO THE POINT WHERE nature is allowed to take care of itself – is a sustainability buzzword. Research from The Wildlife Trusts (*wildlifetrusts.org*), among others, has declared a call to arms, suggesting that if we can protect and restore 30% of land and sea by 2030, we will have done enough to reverse mass extinction caused by climate change. Journeys with Purpose (*journeyswithpurpose.org*) offers travellers the chance to visit some of the world's most revolutionary rewilding projects and learn hands-on skills directly from those dedicated to changing the trajectory of this planet. Check out their trip to Argentina's Iberá National Park, where efforts to tempt jaguars back to the wetlands are making inroads.

52

GIVE TOUR OPERATORS A GRILLING

NOT ALL INDIGENOUS COMMUNITIES HAVE THE CAPACITY OR DESIRE TO set up their own tourism initiatives and booking through a responsible operator can be a great way to learn from their unique way of life while helping them improve their livelihoods. But how do you know if an operator is exploiting Indigenous people? The trick is asking questions, and lots of them, before booking. A few ideas to get you going are: how is the community being remunerated for your trip? What's being done to protect their land rights and environmental resources? Will your guide be local? For further reading, consult the World Tourism Organization's (*e-unwto.org*) Recommendations on Sustainable Development of Indigenous Tourism.

53

WHY IS SLUM TOURISM SO DARN COMPLICATED?

SLUM TOURISM, ALSO KNOWN AS POVERTY TOURISM, OR GHETTO tourism, is one of the more controversial forms of experiential travel. Critics say slum tours allow exploitative companies to make an easy buck by selling poverty porn. Advocates say it provides the people who need it most with income and raises awareness about the problems often-marginalised communities face. We say, slum tourism can be ethical as long as it directly includes residents and profits go towards improving their lives. Take Casa Kolacho (*facebook.com/LaCasaKolacho*), a group of rap and graffiti artists who show tourists around Comuna 13 in Medellín, Colombia. The tour focuses on street art – in particular, their own memorial to fallen friends – and profits fund hip-hop workshops in the local youth centre.

SHARE YOUR DIGITAL KNOW-HOW

YOU MAY NOT CONSIDER YOURSELF A TECH GURU BUT ALL THOSE HOURS on social media, ordering Deliveroo and attending Zoom meetings add up. Many people from the Western world have super-developed digital skills, so have a think about how you can share that knowledge while travelling. Worldpackers (*worldpackers.com*) connects travellers with hosts offering free accommodation in exchange for volunteer work and many are looking for help with their social media, website copy and content creation. Making their digital presence more enticing for your fellow travellers could have a huge impact on their business.

55

LEAVE MORE THAN FOOTPRINTS

THE POPULAR ADAGE, 'TAKE NOTHING BUT PHOTOS, LEAVE NOTHING BUT
footprints' is a good place to start when it comes to desert trips, but
your holiday also has the potential to do a tremendous amount of good.
Sustainable tourism provides a lifeline to people who live in some of the
world's most forbidding landscapes – as long as they are receiving the
profits, of course. For example, in Douz, Tunisia, local camel drivers will lead
you through the Sahara's tawny dunes to the Ksar Ghilane oasis where you'll
cool off in a thermal pool before bedding down at a traditional Bedouin
camp. Fossil–fuel guzzling activities like dune bashing (zooming around in
a 4x4) disrupt the desert's delicate ecosystem and are unlikely to be a local
initiative, so ditch these in favour of something more authentic.

JOIN BEACH CLEANS

WHEN A DEAD WHALE WASHED UP IN SONGKHLA PROVINCE, THAILAND, with 80 plastic bags in its stomach in 2018 it was a sobering moment for many. Yet it's hardly surprising given that there are thought to be 13,000 pieces of plastic litter on every square kilometre of ocean. However, arguably it's the plastic you don't see that poses the greatest threat. Over time, plastic waste becomes brittle and breaks down into tiny particles known as micro or nano-plastics, which change the water's chemical balance and end up being ingested by every living creature – including humans. As well as limiting your own plastic use and recycling, taking part in beach cleans is a great way to do your bit and many coastal communities have their own initiatives. Trashpackers (*trashpackers.org*) is a global movement that encourages travellers to carry a small rubbish bag with them and clean beaches as they go before recording it online to help scientists tackle the problem at the source, while Precious Plastic (*preciousplastic.com*) has a huge database of ideas for how to alchemise waste into something useful.

UNDERSTAND THE CORAL CODE

CORALS MAY LOOK LIKE PLANTS OR ROCKS BUT THEY'RE ACTUALLY evolutionary cousins of jellyfish and are classed as animals. They protect themselves from infection with a mucus layer that is home to a rich microbiome – if brushed by a hand or even a flipper it triggers a stress response that sees the coral eject its zooxanthellae (the photosynthesising micro-organisms that make it colourful) and turn white, also known as coral bleaching. Make sure you practise your finning technique before heading to the reef so you don't end up having a costly accident.

GET HIGH ON THE OCEAN'S SUPPLY

FREE DIVING WITH WHALE SHARKS IN SRI LANKA, SURFING JEFFREYS BAY in South Africa (home to the infamous Supertubes break) and parasailing in Uttarakhand, India — the mighty deep offers more than enough adrenaline-raising experiences. There's no need to take part in water sports that burn fossil fuels and disturb wildlife with noisy motors.

59

TRY REEF-SAFE SUNSCREEN

BEWARE SNORKELLERS: MOST SUNSCREEN CONTAINS HARMFUL chemicals that seep into the water when you swim and interfere with coral's reproduction and growth cycles. Unfortunately, the term 'reef-friendly' isn't regulated and you'll find many brands using it, despite the fact their products contain nasties like oxybenzone, octinoxate and octocrylene. The answer is rash vests and micro-sized (or non-nano) mineral sunscreens. Check out Save the Reef (*savethereef.org*) for further details.

DO DOLPHIN WATCHING RIGHT

THEY LOVE TO SURF AND CHATTER, TRAVEL IN TIGHT-KNIT FAMILY groups and have the longest memories in the animal kingdom, so it's little surprise that dolphins have long fascinated us humans. And we do mean 'long'. The desert city of Petra, believed to have been established in 312 BC, has images of dolphins carved into the rock. When dolphin spotting, steer clear of operators that guarantee encounters as this probably means they are luring them in with food, which is a big no-no. Instead, look out for those with accreditation from the World Cetacean Alliance (*worldcetaceanalliance.org*) and ensure they turn off the boat's motor if any dolphins do show up.

61

HOW TO SPOT AN
ETHICAL ANIMAL SANCTUARY

THE BADDIES WHO RUN SINISTER SANCTUARIES THAT EXPLOIT WILDLIFE have got hold of words like 'ethical' and 'sustainable', so we need to be more discerning than ever. A great place to start is the Global Federation of Animal Sanctuaries' (*sanctuaryfederation.org*) extensive list of accredited sanctuaries that meet strict welfare standards. However, there are plenty of great operations that don't have an accreditation, and in these cases, you can glean lots of clues from their website and social media. If visitors are invited to volunteer, they should only be doing things like chopping food and mucking out enclosures rather than touching animals. Visiting hours should also be limited to avoid too much disruption.

WALK THIS WAY

WALKING WITH EVERYTHING YOU NEED ON YOUR BACK IS FREEDOM IN ITS purest form. Here are two simple ways to be a more responsible hiker.

- **Be prepared** – If you aren't covering all bases, you're more likely to put pressure on local resources as well as extra strain on the environment. Pack eco-friendly toiletries, more food and water than you need and gear that'll see you through the worst conditions. As walker Alfred Wainwright wrote: 'There's no such thing as bad weather, only unsuitable clothing.'

- **Deal with waste** – The rule, 'Carry it in, carry it out' unfortunately includes feminine hygiene products, food wrappers and toilet paper. If you're on a multi-day trek staying at remote teahouses or camps (like Uganda's Mountains of the Moon route) it may still be best to take your rubbish with you so you can dispose of it responsibly. Looks like gallon-sized resealable freezer bags are your new best friend.

63

ENGAGE WITH A DESTINATION'S DARK SIDE

VISITING SITES OF ATROCITY SUCH AS CAMBODIA'S KILLING FIELDS OR Auschwitz may sound like a grisly addition to an itinerary but 'dark tourism', as it's sometimes known, can be an important way to understand another culture. The key to doing it ethically is in your intention — presumably to honour the dead and learn from the past rather than gawp and take controversial selfies. If locals appear to want to talk, listen, ask sensitive questions, and avoid giving your own opinion.

BURN BABY BURN

CHANGING THE WORLD CAN FEEL LIKE SUCH A HERCULEAN TASK THAT IT can be tempting to throw in the towel before even getting started. Yet there is often an easier way to achieve your sustainability goals. For example, efficient cookstoves rather than open fires are a cheap, simple way to support the health of millions of people, all while keeping children in school rather than out looking for firewood. In the Serengeti, Maasai women are leading the way with the Maasai Clean Cookstoves Project. When you book to visit them through G Adventures (*gadventures.com*), a percentage of your fee goes directly to the project.

65

HOW TO BE A HAPPY SNAPPER

IF YOU'RE EXPLORING KYOTO'S GION DISTRICT, BE CAREFUL WHERE YOU point your lens. Visitors who take pictures of geishas without their consent can be fined Y10,000. Many countries have rules around what can be photographed, while in others local people may have personal reasons for not wanting to be in front of a camera. A few golden rules for more ethical travel photography are:

- ◆ **Always ask permission** – A smile and gesture is often enough.
- ◆ **Offer remuneration** – It may feel weird to suggest money but it's only fair, particularly if someone has taken the time to pose. Buying whatever they're selling is another good way to show your appreciation.
- ◆ **Share your snap** – Offer to share the image with them and if they say yes, make sure you keep your word.

TIP#
66

HELP KEEP SACRED SITES SACRED

WHETHER IT IS A MAN-MADE PHENOMENON SUCH AS BARCELONA'S
Sagrada Familia or a natural attraction such as central Australia's Uluru,
sacred sites should be treated with respect. Investigate the customs
before you go to avoid faux pas like wearing the wrong thing or taking
pictures where it's not allowed. The documentaries *In the Light of
Reverence* and *Standing on Sacred Ground* both highlight American Indian
struggles to protect their sacred places and are an enlightening watch. For
more thought-provoking information and advice, try Sacred Sites International
Foundation (*sacred-sites.org*).

67

UNLEASH YOUR INNER SCIENTIST

COLLECTING DATA IS ONE OF THE MOST VITAL AND TIME-CONSUMING aspects of conservation but many hands make light work. Citizen science comes in the form of picking up and registering data on litter, recording butterfly sightings, or monitoring marine flotsam – all you need is a phone and the internet. Look out for these initiatives as you traverse the globe:

- **FrogID** (*frogid.net.au*) – On a mission to protect Australia's declining frog population, this database asks users to record frog calls, identify them on the app and note the species.
- **Planet Patrol** (*planetpatrol.co*) – A global community working on a giant survey of inland litter pollution. Simply take pictures of rubbish when you're out and about and upload them to the app (before picking it up, of course!).
- **Globe at Night** (*globeatnight.org*) – One for the night owls, this international project asks volunteers to measure the brightness of the night sky so scientists can build up a picture of light pollution.

MAKE EVERY DAY MARKET DAY

LIFE'S TOUGH FOR SMALL-SCALE FARMERS AND GETTING TOUGHER AS global warming causes more extreme weather conditions but putting food on our plates depends on them. In fact, small-scale farmers produce more than 70% of the world's food, according to the UN Food and Agriculture Organization. Show farmers some love by eating in restaurants that shout about their suppliers (such as The Bull Inn in Totnes, England) and do your shopping at farmer's markets. After all, San Marzano tomatoes taste even better when bought from Naples' Mercato Pignasecca... learning how to choose the best by copying local nonne is a bonus.

69

THINK ON YOUR 'FOODPRINT'

EVERY MEAL WE EAT HAS A 'FOODPRINT' (THE ENVIRONMENTAL IMPACT OF the process it takes to get the food from farm to fork) and, due simply to geography, some destinations have a bigger impact than others. Take the 1,192 tiny islands that make up the Maldives. The 'soil' is mostly crushed coral, meaning most resort meals are flown in. When visiting, research what ingredients can be produced locally and stick to those where possible or book a hotel that grows its own food. Soneva Fushi, for example, turns kitchen scraps into yummy compost for its organic garden.

A TIP ON TIPPING

TIPPING IS A GREAT WAY OF ENSURING CASH FROM YOUR TRIP GOES straight into local pockets, as well as a chance to subsidise wages. However, do a little research first into what is deemed an appropriate amount (if in doubt, 10% is generally a safe bet). Over-tipping can upset society's delicate balance. In Cuba, taxi drivers earn far more than doctors meaning the brightest brainboxes tend to emigrate overseas leaving the medical system chronically short staffed.

SCALE IT DOWN

WE GET IT. SAVOURING SEAFOOD AT A WATERFRONT RESTAURANT screams 'holiday', particularly when paired with a bottle of crisp white. However, the Marine Stewardship Council says a third of fish stocks are fished beyond their sustainable limits, putting the whole world's food security at risk. Scour Seafood Watch (*seafoodwatch.org*) to check you're munching on replenishable species, and don't be afraid to ask questions about how and where your meal was caught. 'Local fishermen using hook-and-line methods' is the response you want to hear. Bottom trawling means scooping up every living thing in a boat's wake, as well as stirring up all the carbon that's stored in the ocean floor.

TELL FOOD WASTE TO F*CK OFF

A CHILD DIES OF HUNGER EVERY 30 SECONDS, SO WASTING FOOD IS A no-no for ethical travellers. Food waste is also a major cause of greenhouse gases. Depending on your location, use apps like Olio (*olioex.com*), Too Good to Go (*toogoodtogo.com*) and DamoGO (*damogo.co*) to score free and discounted meals.

73

DON'T BEGRUDGE PAYING MORE

WE'VE ALL BEEN THERE: ORDERING A COFFEE AND FEELING OUTRAGED for having been charged far more than the regular in front of us. An unofficial 'tourist tax' can be irksome but try to see it as a way of redistributing wealth and making sure locals benefit economically from your visit. Much of tourism is seasonal and, as we've seen from Covid-19, it can be unreliable, so you can't blame people for building in a little extra padding – especially in countries where the average salary is far less than your own.

KEEP UP THE GOOD WORK ON WASTE

WHEN IT COMES TO PICKING RESTAURANTS, DOING AS LOCALS DO IS almost always good advice. But this isn't necessarily true when it comes to disposing of waste. Some countries still don't have a culture of recycling. It's particularly important to keep up your good habits in these places if you can and to ask hotels and restaurants where the recycling facilities are. Even if they don't have any, it could start a conversation or prompt them to consider it.

75

RECONSIDER THE HAGGLE

SURE, EVERYONE LOVES A BARGAIN, BUT REMEMBER THAT 800 MILLION people earn less than $1.25 a day – that's more than Europe's entire population. You probably won't notice if you spend an extra 60 Moroccan dirhams on beautiful leather babouches (slippers), but a stallholder could feed their family for several days with that money. Pay cash to those who need it most, as many people in developing economies live hand-to-mouth.

GIVE WHERE IT COUNTS

PICTURE THE SCENE: YOU'RE WALKING DOWN A STREET AND ARE suddenly surrounded by barefoot children, plucking at your sleeve and asking for money. It feels heart-wrenching to turn them down, but many have been lured away from their parents by traffickers and anything you give them will only encourage this brutal trade to grow. It's better to support little ones by donating to international NGOs such as Street Child United (*streetchildunited.org*) or UNICEF (*unicef.org*).

77

FEELING CRAFTY?

KEEP YOUR EYES PEELED WHEN VISITING CRAFT WORKSHOPS. THOSE young people diligently painting paper lanterns could be children being forced into work rather than the enthusiastic apprentices the salesperson is no doubt keen to describe them as. Take stock of the working conditions. Ask yourself if the workers look engrossed in their work or too scared to stop. If you're not convinced, don't part with any of your cash and be sure to report it to your tour company or guide.

SAY 'NON MERCI' TO MASS-PRODUCED SOUVENIRS

PARIS: THE CITY OF LIGHTS, LOVE AND... EIFFEL TOWER KEYCHAINS.
Anyone who has been to Paris will have seen these small, spiky statuettes, often sold for as little as €1 and prone to breaking, before inevitably finding their way to landfill. They're flown in from China and typically peddled by illegal immigrants, who risk arrest for very little income. The same goes for I Heart NY T-shirts, mini Colosseums, and plastic magnets in just about any city in the world. Instead, opt for locally made mementos such as handicrafts, food and vintage homewares. Or, even better, preserve your memories through photos or a journal, and then you can visit Paris any time you like.

79

IF IT *IS* BROKE...

SEE IF A LOCAL CAN HELP MEND IT! WHEN TRAVEL EQUIPMENT GIVES UP on the road, always try to find a fixer rather than chucking it, particularly if you're somewhere without many municipal waste facilities. People living in destinations where resources are harder to come by may well have the skills to bring even the weariest possessions back to life.

80

CLOSE THE LOOP

CRADLE-TO-CRADLE OR CLOSED-LOOP ECONOMIES ARE THE HOLY GRAIL when it comes to responsible consumption. Essentially it means using things again and again, often in different iterations, rather than buying them, using them and chucking them, which is currently the standard model. Hotels like Conscious Hotel Westerpark (*conscioushotels.com*) in Amsterdam and London's Inhabit (*inhabithotels.com*) are wising up to this by filling their rooms with furniture and amenities that fulfil this criteria, as are small companies like Davy J (*davyj.com*) and Salomé Swim (*salomeswim.com*), both of which design swimwear made from old fishing nets.

81

OPEN YOUR MIND
TO ALTERNATIVE MEDICINE

IF SOMETHING GOES WRONG ON YOUR TRAVELS, YOU SHOULD OF COURSE seek the appropriate healthcare but be open-minded about local practices too. Consulting an ayurvedic healer in India or an acupuncturist in China will give you a unique insight into local culture, as well as allowing you to support the community rather than big pharma. Many alternative treatments are far more holistic than Western medicine; a chi nei tsang session (emotion-releasing abdominal massage) in Thailand, for example, will leave you feeling mentally, as well as physically lighter.

TIP#

82

TACKLE RACISM ON THE ROAD

THE REALITY IS THAT THE COLOUR OF SOMEONE'S SKIN CAN HAVE BOTH positive and negative impacts on their experience while travelling. Because the vast majority of travel writers in Australia, the US and Europe are white – a hangover from the industry's roots in upper-class male explorers sending dispatches home – they often can only portray their own experiences. Some must-read travel writers of colour include Oneika Raymond, Sarah Khan, Danielle Pointdujour and James Edward Mills, whose book, *The Adventure Gap: Changing the Face of the Outdoors*, chronicles the first all-black summit attempt on Alaska's Mount Denali.

83

CLEAN YOUR CONSCIENCE AS WELL AS YOUR CLOTHES

IN EVERY COUNTRY IN THE WORLD, WOMEN CONTINUE TO BE PAID LESS than men – when they're paid at all. Women spend an average of three to six hours on unpaid work every day, with men clocking in at between half an hour and two hours. Rather than using your hotel's laundry service, head out and support a local instead. In countries such as Vietnam and Laos, women living in tourist districts often have signs on their doors saying that they wash clothes; if they have to shoulder the domestic burden, it's only right they earn some cash while they're at it. Remember to ask them not to tumble dry your clothes as this takes five times as much energy as one load of washing.

CELEBRATE OTHER GENDERS

EXISTING LEGISLATION IN MOST COUNTRIES CAN LEAD TO SOME TRICKY questions at borders for transgender and non-binary people. So far, only seven countries have adjusted the rules to allow citizens to change the gender on their passport to 'X': Canada, Argentina, Australia, Denmark, Iceland, Nepal and New Zealand. Although Western culture may still consider gender fluidity a new concept, it has been part of life for centuries around the world:

- **Muxes, Mexico** – Based in the small town of Juchitán de Zaragoza in southern Oaxaca State, muxes are generally born in a male body but identify as neither female nor male. They're celebrated every year with a festival called *Vela de Las Intrepidas* (Vigil of the Intrepids).
- **Fa'afafines and Fa'afatamas, Samoa** – Fluid gender roles that move between male and female worlds, Fa'afafines and Fa'afatamas traditionally play an important role in educating fellow Samoans about sex.

85

SWITCH OFF

DID YOU KNOW THAT THE ENERGY REQUIRED TO KEEP SERVERS RUNNING for cloud storage is similar to the aviation industry in terms of the amount of greenhouse gases it releases? On top of this, a one-minute mobile-to-mobile call produces 0.1 g of CO_2, a text 0.014 g of CO_2 and 1 GB of data uses 0.3 kg of CO_2. We all know that our screen time can creep up on holiday thanks to all the snaps, map use and calls home. Opting for a digital detox is not only greener, but it will also let you be more present on your holiday.

LOOK FOR INNOVATION
OF ALL KINDS

SOMETIMES INNOVATION INVOLVES COMPLEX SCIENTIFIC RESEARCH (À LA developing new vaccines) and other times it means painting everything purple. Banwol Island, an impoverished fishing community off the coast of South Korea, recently transformed itself into an attraction for Instagram-loving travellers by painting 400 houses purple and planting rolling lavender fields for good measure. In 2021, the United Nations World Tourism Organization (*unwto.org*) launched the 'Best Tourism Villages' initiative to celebrate innovation in rural communities that helps to progress the SDGs.

87

BE A BETTER ALLY TO TRAVELLERS WITH DISABILITIES

ABLE-BODIED TRAVELLERS CAN HELP MAKE TRAVEL ACCESSIBLE FOR everyone by holding hotels and tour companies to account. If a brand doesn't have an accessibility policy on their website, ask about this when booking. The more customers make it clear that this is something they expect, the more quickly brands will step into line. Educate yourself by reading and amplifying the voices of explorers with disabilities such as Catarina Rivera (*@blindishlatina*) and Cory Lee (*@curbfreecorylee*).

88

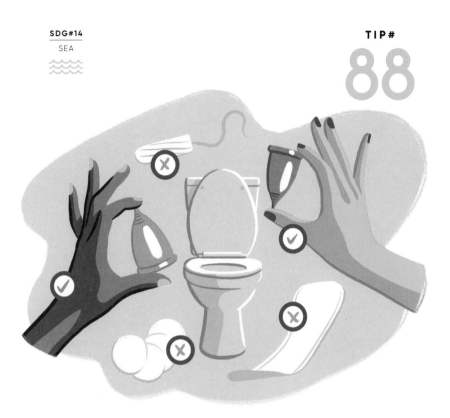

BE MINDFUL OF WHAT YOU FLUSH

FLUSHING THINGS LIKE WET WIPES AND TAMPONS OFTEN FEELS LIKE A fuss-free solution to getting rid of waste. However, both are usually made, at least partly, of synthetic plastics, and have an uncanny ability to dodge water treatment plants and sneak into the ocean. If you have to use them, make sure you bin rather than flush. Far better, find re-usable alternatives such as menstrual cups and makeup remover pads made of bamboo.

89

MAKE MOZZIES BUZZ OFF

VERY FEW ANIMALS CAN COMPETE WITH MOSQUITOES WHEN IT COMES TO body size versus potential to annoy ratio. The most effective sprays contain Deet, which was invented in America in the forties as an agricultural pesticide and is toxic to many animals and plants. So, is it always a no-no? Well, that depends on where you're travelling. If it is somewhere mosquitoes carry diseases like malaria, dengue fever and zika virus, you probably don't want to take any chances with your health. However, if the mosquitoes aren't dangerous, there are plenty of alternative ways to prevent bites that are gentler on the environment. Try:

* wearing loose, flowing clothing that covers your arms and legs;
* sleeping under a net;
* using natural repellents that contain lemon eucalyptus (these need to be re-applied every hour);
* citronella candles; and
* ensuring there are no puddles of water near your accommodation where mozzies can breed.

MIND YOUR PS AND QS

BURPING AT THE DINNER TABLE IN AUSTRALIA IS RUDE BUT IN CHINA IT'S the highest compliment. In Ethiopia, eating with one's left hand is disrespectful, while in Mongolia stepping on someone's foot is a sign you're spoiling for a fight. As well as these smaller cultural quirks, hierarchical communication, gender norms and attitudes towards punctuality all differ vastly from place to place, so brushing up on etiquette before you arrive will help you avoid misunderstandings and endear you to your hosts.

TREAT LOCALS WITH DIGNITY

HOW DO WE NAVIGATE POWER IMBALANCES WHEN WE TRAVEL? IT'S A complicated issue, particularly if you're from a culture that has historically oppressed that of your hosts. However, one thing we *can* do is acknowledge the humanity of locals and go out of our way to treat them with dignity. Stand back and let them go first, hold doors open, listen and, when we get home, avoid reductive generalities like 'the people were so gentle' as these often have their roots in colonial perceptions.

REMEMBER, SELF-CARE
IS HEALTHCARE

WHILE THIS BOOK IS ALL ABOUT LOOKING OUTWARDS, NO ONE CAN BE A
truly responsible traveller if they aren't looking after themselves too. How can
you help others if you're tired, hungry, permanently hungover and anxious?
While travel is all about freedom, having a daily routine based around healthy
habits can be a game changer and make the feelings of loneliness that every
traveller grapples with at some point far easier to manage. Think going to
bed fairly early, getting up around 8am, starting the day with a mindfulness
practice, making time for physical exercise, eating healthily 80% of the time
and journalling a few times a week. Apps like Headspace, FreeMind and
Insight Timer all have extensive libraries of free meditations.

TIP#

93

SDG#13

CLIMATE

STAY LONGER

WAIT, WAIT, WAIT. NOT SO FAST. RATHER THAN TAKING MULTIPLE micro-trips a year, try going away less often and for longer. Not only does this save on carbon emissions from flights, but it also allows you to connect with a destination in a more meaningful way. Many employers are far more flexible on working from home since the Covid-19 pandemic and as long as you have good internet, it's very possible to work from the road. So why not ask? The worst they can do is say no.

HOME SWEET HOME

THEY MAY NOT HAVE QUITE THE GLAMOUR OF LONG-DISTANCE TRAVEL, but staycations are one of the most sustainable holidays out there. Aside from the obvious carbon savings on air travel, they're also a chance to redistribute wealth within your home country by visiting less prosperous areas – many of which are often the most isolated and therefore also the most beautiful. And there's a lot to be said for not having to kill time in airports.

95

PASS IT ON

WHEN THE TIME COMES TO GO HOME, LOOK AT YOUR STUFF THROUGH A local's eyes. Is there anything that could make a useful gift? Items like sanitary products, clothes, books, over-the-counter medicines and sun cream can all be far harder to get hold of in certain countries so your hosts may really appreciate them. Make sure they're clean and left in a neat pile in your room with a thank you note to be discovered after you've gone.

BEWARE SNEAKY SEEDS

EVEN TRAVELLERS WHO ARE CAREFUL TO TREAD LIGHTLY CAN END UP
unwittingly transporting invasive species on their shoes and gear. In Australia,
phytophthora (root rot) spread in soil on walkers' boots is causing havoc
for native plants, while didymo (or 'rock snot') – which hitches rides on wet
fishing gear – has devastated riverbeds in New Zealand. Make sure you
give your boots, bag wheels, bikes and car a good scrub before leaving a
destination. If you want to be extra safe, carry a small bottle of disinfectant to
spray on the soles of your shoes just before entering a protected area.

BECOME A DIGITAL NOMAD

WE MAY NOT FEEL LIKE WE HAVE MUCH TO THANK THE COVID-19 pandemic for (particularly when it comes to travel) but it changed the nature of work forever. Industries that would have sworn they could never function remotely found ways of coping, often by embracing technology and platforms such as Zoom and Slack. This has given many people far more freedom to travel. Meanwhile, more than 45 countries now offer visas allowing foreign professionals to stay for an extended period without paying income tax. Brazil, Cape Verde and Georgia all have excellent internet coverage and competitive living costs – why settle for a homemade sandwich when you could be trying *satsivi* (Georgian stew) for the first time?

MAKE THEM PROUD BY BEING LOUD

DOING THE RIGHT THING IS SO MUCH MORE FUN WHEN OTHER PEOPLE recognise the effort we're putting in, right? When hotels and tour operators shout about their equal-opportunity recruitment policies, make sure you take to the rooftops – or internet – to spread the word. Lavish them with praise on social media. Leave glowing Tripadvisor reviews online. Not only does this encourage their efforts, if competitors see that customers care, they're more likely to follow suit.

99

BECOME PART OF THE MOVEMENT

WE'RE ALWAYS LOOKING TO LEARN, WHICH IS WHY WE'RE LEAVING THE final tip up to you. What resonates with you? What inspires you to travel smarter, more ethically? Write your tip and share it on Instagram with the hashtag #ethicaltraveller. Is this a thinly veiled marketing ploy? Well, yes and no. Sure, we're looking to sell books, but we also truly believe ethical tourism will help save the world, one traveller at a time.

ADD
YOUR OWN
SDG

Smith Street Books

Published in 2022 by Smith Street Books

Naarm | Melbourne | Australia

smithstreetbooks.com

ISBN: 978-1-92581-198-8

Publisher: Paul McNally

Project editor: Aisling Coughlan

Editor: Kate Symons

Design, layout and illustrations: Julia Murray

Proofreader: Pamela Dunne

Printed & bound in China by C&C Offset Printing Co., Ltd.

Book 223

10 9 8 7 6 5 4 3 2 1

MIX
Paper from
responsible sources
FSC® C008047